WORMS & WORMING

by
Russell Lyon BVM&S, MRCVS

Illustrations by
Carole Vincer

KENILWORTH PRESS

First published in Great Britain by
Kenilworth Press, an imprint of Quiller Publishing Ltd

British Library Cataloguing in Publication Data
A catalogue record for this book is available from the British Library

ISBN 978-1-905693-06-1

Printed in Great Britain by Halstan & Co. Ltd

Disclaimer of Liability
The author and publisher shall have neither liability nor
responsibility to any person or entity with respect to any loss or
damage caused or alleged to be caused directly or indirectly by the
information contained in this book. While the book is as accurate as
the authors can make it, there may be errors, omissions and
inaccuracies.

KENILWORTH PRESS
An imprint of Quiller Publishing Ltd
Wykey House, Wykey, Shrewsbury, SY4 1JA
tel: 01939 261616 fax: 01939 261606
e-mail: info@quillerbooks.com
website: www.kenilworthpress.co.uk

CONTENTS

INTRODUCTION

Intestinal parasites (worms) have been present in horses and ponies as long as equines have existed. These parasites vary enormously and often have very different life cycles. They can be as diverse and different as a sheep is different from a dog or a flea from a frog, and are classified according to their 'life-style'. Some might be recognised in the dung of the affected animal but many – especially the most dangerous worms – lay eggs that cannot be seen with the naked eye.

Horse owners are aware that their animals have worms and should be wormed on a regular basis. Some people may use a wormer twice a year, and others with almost religious fervour use one every six weeks winter and summer 'whether the horse needs it or not'. Both approaches could be equally inappropriate for the health of the animal.

Worming drugs – anthelmintics – are essential for the health of your horse but they should be used correctly, at the right time and at the right dose, or you might just as well chuck your money on the muck-heap! Many horse owners are also aware that they should not use the same product on their animals all the time in case the worms become drug resistant. They will use a different preparation every time, which can be quite the wrong thing to do. Horse owners and horses are very fortunate that today there is a wide range of very effective drugs that can be used against internal parasitism, but no one drug is effective against all types of parasite.

What is certain is that no two situations are the same: what may be the correct worming regime for one horse owner or in one livery yard may not be right for another just a few miles away. An older horse grazing in a field of twenty acres with one other companion and a few sheep will be at much less risk than a youngster in a six-acre paddock with many others for company.

Horse owners need to think about what they are doing and consult with their vet to work out a treatment and parasite prevention programme. Many, unfortunately, still select one or two wormers, which a friend may 'swear by' as the best or which can be bought at a very good price. There still seem to be more misconceptions about wormers and worming than almost any other type of equine medication. I don't know of any statistics to back my assertion, but I know from personal experience of working with horses that many hundreds of animals in the UK and many thousands all over the world die preventable deaths from the effects of internal parasites. In this day and age this should not happen. Make sure it does not happen to your horse or pony.

ROUNDWORMS (NEMATODES)

Roundworms (Nematodes) are the most common internal parasite in the horse. They all have a round cylindrical form, tapering at either end like earthworms, but most of them are very much smaller and are further subdivided into:

Large Redworms – Strongyles

Strongylus vulgaris, *S. edentatus* and *S. equinus* are just three of over fifty species of this type. They are also known as **redworms** or bloodworms as they are dark red in colour. They vary in size between 1.5cm and 5cm in length but will seldom be seen except when an animal has just been treated with a wormer, when the adults might be observed being passed in the dung. As part of the normal life cycle, eggs, which can only be seen with a microscope, are laid by the adult parasite. These mature into larvae in two or three days while in the dung and then migrate onto the pasture and are consumed as the horse grazes. The larvae mature in the gut and burrow into the arteries supplying the bowel. As a consequence they can cause obstruction to blood vessels supplying the bowel, and severe bouts of colic.

Horses and ponies with heavy strongyle infestations will lose weight, become anaemic and, if the bowel arteries become blocked, can suffer a severe and often fatal colic. It is also possible that an animal could quite suddenly bleed to death if a mesenteric artery bursts. It's incredible to think that an animal as big as a horse can be killed by a worm that is a couple of centimetres long.

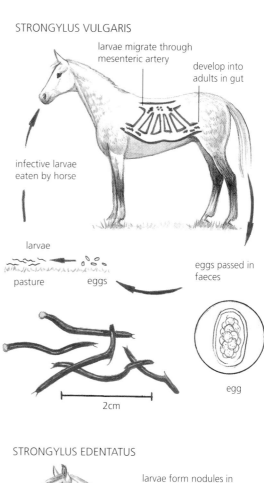

STRONGYLUS VULGARIS

larvae migrate through mesenteric artery

develop into adults in gut

infective larvae eaten by horse

larvae

pasture   eggs

eggs passed in faeces

egg

2cm

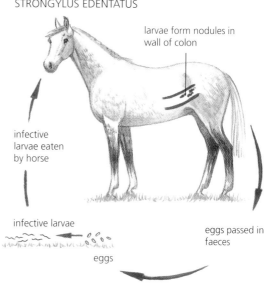

STRONGYLUS EDENTATUS

larvae form nodules in wall of colon

infective larvae eaten by horse

infective larvae

eggs

eggs passed in faeces

ROUNDWORMS (NEMATODES) CONT.

Small Redworms – Small Strongyles

These are also known as cyathostomes and there are over forty species worldwide. Larvae burrow into the intestinal wall where (encysted) they can lie dormant for up to two years. Typically they re-emerge as adults at the end of winter, when the animal is more vulnerable, and can cause severe damage to the gut wall. Profound weight loss will be seen, along with watery diarrhoea and colic. Death is not uncommon in younger animals. Less severe infestation will result in a loss of condition, a dry, staring coat and a pot-belly. Infected animals usually have poor appetites. Even if it survives, a youngster may never fully recover condition due to internal damage. Small redworms are most likely to be resistant to drug treatment, especially to those from the Benzimidazole group.

Large Roundworms – Ascarids

In the UK these will be *Parascaris equorum*. They look like large white earthworms and might be seen in the dung when a youngster matures (at around nine months, when it is not uncommon for them to be passed in the dung as the animal self-cures) or after a worming treatment. The adult worm lives in the small intestine and produces large numbers of tough-coated eggs (up to 200,000 a day!). These are microscopic in size and very infective to foals. Worm eggs can be found – but cannot be seen by the naked eye – sticking to the coat and udder of the lactating mare. The infection is usually acquired from pasture, hay or water that has been contaminated by dung from other horses, including the mother. The life cycle,

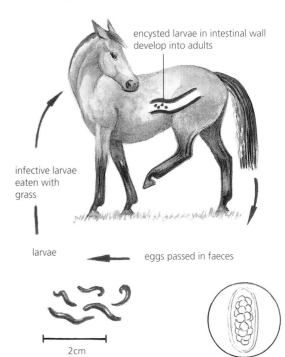

CYATHOSTOMES

encysted larvae in intestinal wall develop into adults

infective larvae eaten with grass

larvae

eggs passed in faeces

2cm

egg

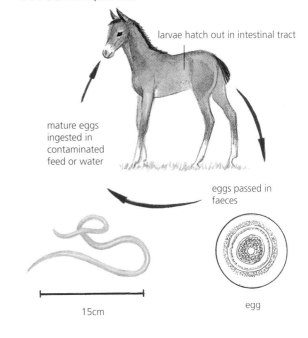

PARASCARIS EQUORUM

larvae hatch out in intestinal tract

mature eggs ingested in contaminated feed or water

eggs passed in faeces

15cm

egg

from the first eggs being ingested by the foal to the adult worms maturing and laying eggs in the small intestine, takes only two to three months. These adults can block and even rupture a small intestine with fatal consequences. Even if the worm burden is not fatal it can result in weight loss and general debility due to anaemia, diarrhoea and colic. During the worms' migratory phase they pass through the lungs where the larvae can cause coughing and sometimes pneumonia.

Stomach Hair Worms – Trichostrongylus axei

The adult worm is very small and difficult to see with the naked eye. In the horse the time from ingesting infective larvae to becoming adult and shedding eggs is only about twenty-five days. The parasite is probably more significant in Australia, when symptoms are seen in the spring. In the UK worms are more likely to cause irritation to the stomach in summer and autumn. Heavy infestations can cause rapid weight loss and diarrhoea, but the parasite is easily treated.

Neck Threadworms – Onchocerca species

These are slender worms (adults 2–6cm in length) that lie tightly curled in small nodules in the neck ligaments, and less obviously in the ligaments and tendons in the lower legs. They are found all over the world, but most surveys indicate a higher incidence in the USA (53%) than the UK (23%). The biting midge is the intermediate host for the infective larvae of this worm. The worms rarely cause a problem, but at one time it was thought they might be implicated in the condition called fistulous withers (although this has never been proved). The average

horse owner will never see signs of this parasite except occasionally after dosing the horse with an Ivermectin preparation, when dying microfilaria (immature Onchocerca parasites) will provoke a local reaction on the skin of the neck.

TRICHOSTRONGYLUS AXEI

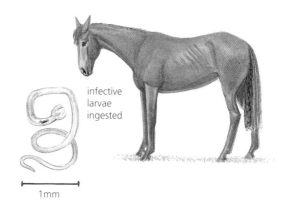

infective larvae ingested

1mm

ONCHOCERCA SPECIES

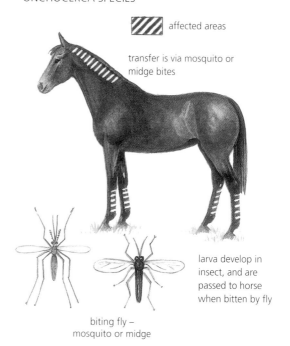

affected areas

transfer is via mosquito or midge bites

larva develop in insect, and are passed to horse when bitten by fly

biting fly – mosquito or midge

ROUNDWORMS (NEMATODES) CONT.

Pinworms – Oxyuris equi These parasites are very common, but are more irritating than dangerous to the horse. They have a worldwide distribution and the adult females are white with pointed tails and can be up to 10cm in length. The male by contrast is only about 1cm. The animal acquires the parasite by consuming contaminated hay, grass, grain or water. The larvae mature in the large intestine in three to four months, then the female sticks her anterior end out of the horse's bottom and lays masses of yellowish-grey gelatinous eggs around the anus. This causes severe irritation, in some cases causing the animal to rub on any available post or stable fitting. The itching can be confused with 'sweet itch' or even lice infestations, but the itch is confined to the hindquarters and instant relief can be obtained by wiping away the eggs from the dock area with a damp, disposable cloth.

Intestinal Threadworms – Strongyloides westeri These parasites, found all over the world, are quite slender, hair-like worms that look like twisted thread. The host animal becomes infected through eating contaminated feed and by grazing. If the weather conditions are moist the larvae can even penetrate the skin. Foals become infected through larvae excreted in the mother's milk. Young animals develop diarrhoea, lose weight or have a reduced growth rate. The diarrhoea can be confused with scouring associated with hormonal changes in the mare's milk when she comes into season.

OXYURIS EQUI

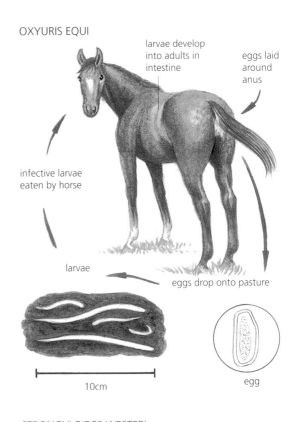

larvae develop into adults in intestine

eggs laid around anus

infective larvae eaten by horse

larvae

eggs drop onto pasture

10cm

egg

STRONGYLOIDES WESTERI

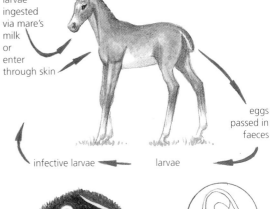

larvae ingested via mare's milk or enter through skin

eggs passed in faeces

infective larvae

larvae

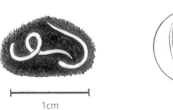

1cm

egg

Lungworms – Dictyocaulis arnfieldi

This parasite has a worldwide distribution but is especially important in temperate climates. Donkeys are the natural host but outward symptoms are unusual. A horse or pony grazing in the same field with an infected donkey may pick up the parasite and develop a hard, hacking cough. This is due to adult worms being present in the bronchi. These can only be seen at post-mortem or by endoscope as small thread-like white worms up to 5cm in length, surrounded by froth, in the air passages of the affected animal. In some situations the larvae migrate from the dung onto the surface of the fungus *Pilobolus*, which has seed capsules that erupt, projecting the larvae up to 3m (even further in windy conditions) onto the surrounding herbage.

Large-mouthed Stomach Worms – Habronema muscae

Although found worldwide this worm is mostly seen in warm countries. Whilst it can irritate the stomach, it more commonly causes summer sores (cutaneous habronemiasis) on the skin of the affected animal, and a persistent eye discharge when the eye is attacked. The symptoms are due to the invasion of the skin or the tissues around the eye by larvae deposited by the flies, not swallowed by the horse. The larvae burrow into the skin causing severe itching and self-inflicted injuries.

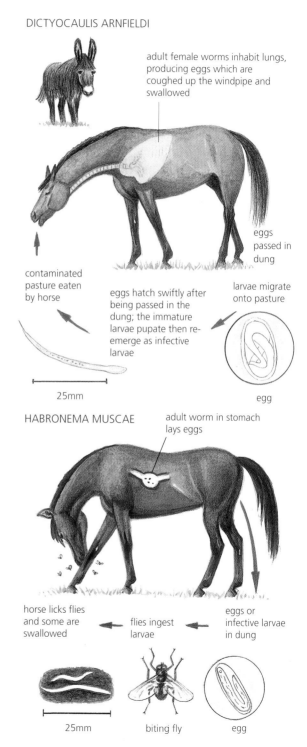

DICTYOCAULIS ARNFIELDI

adult female worms inhabit lungs, producing eggs which are coughed up the windpipe and swallowed

eggs passed in dung

contaminated pasture eaten by horse

eggs hatch swiftly after being passed in the dung; the immature larvae pupate then re-emerge as infective larvae

larvae migrate onto pasture

25mm

egg

HABRONEMA MUSCAE

adult worm in stomach lays eggs

horse licks flies and some are swallowed

flies ingest larvae

eggs or infective larvae in dung

25mm

biting fly

egg

Tapeworms & Liver Fluke (Cestodes & Trematodes)

Tapeworms (Cestodes) These are flat worms, and two types are found in the horse: *Anoplocephala perfoliata*, which is the most common tapeworm, and A. *magna*, which is larger. A. *perfoliata* used to be thought fairly harmless but is now believed to be a major cause of up to 20% of surgical colic cases. It causes irritation, inflammation and ulceration of the lining of the gut. The intermediate host for the worm is the forage mite, which is found on pasture, and on hay and straw during the winter. Thus the horse is exposed to infection all year round, so worming control every six months is vital.

Tapeworm segments can sometimes be seen on the surface of newly passed dung. The absence of segments does not mean that the animal is not infected, and regular treatments or blood tests are advised. The segments disintegrate in the dung, releasing eggs which are ingested by the forage mite. The horse in turn swallows these, and the life cycle is complete in three to five months. Apart from colic, tapeworms cause general unthriftiness and digestive upsets.

Liver fluke (Trematodes) Flukes are flat worms. The most important parasite in this group is *Fasciola hepatica*. It has a small leaf-like shape and when mature is about 3cm in length. Liver fluke is a parasite that requires an intermediate host – the snail, *Limnaea truncatula* in the UK – and these are found in mild, wet conditions.

Liver fluke is rare in horses in the UK but can cause unthriftiness and anaemia. A vet would need to be involved with a diagnosis and treatment.

ANOPLOCEPHALA PERFOLIATA

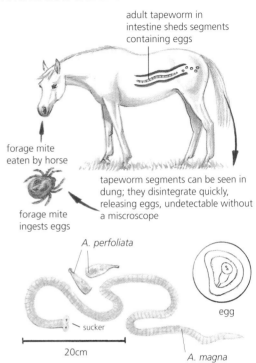

adult tapeworm in intestine sheds segments containing eggs

forage mite eaten by horse

tapeworm segments can be seen in dung; they disintegrate quickly, releasing eggs, undetectable without a miscroscope

forage mite ingests eggs

A. perfoliata

sucker

20cm

egg

A. magna

FASCIOLA HEPATICA

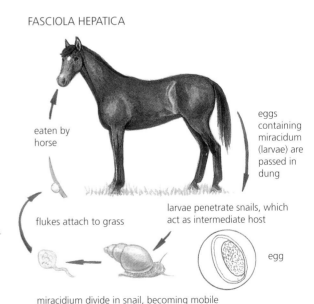

eaten by horse

eggs containing miracidum (larvae) are passed in dung

flukes attach to grass

larvae penetrate snails, which act as intermediate host

egg

miracidium divide in snail, becoming mobile immature fluke (*metacercariae*), then leave snail and attach to grass

BOTS & WARBLES (PSEUDO-WORMS)

Bots Bots are not actually true worms although they look like worms as they develop in the horse's stomach. They are the larval stages of the gasterophilus fly, which has various species with a worldwide distribution. The flies are dark, about 1–2cm long, with transverse bands on the wings. The larvae, when present in the stomach or when passed in the dung, are 1.5–2cm long and reddish orange in colour. They look like large maggots. In temperate climates the flies are active in the late summer when they cause horses and ponies great annoyance and lay eggs on the hairs of the forelegs and shoulders. These flies are very common and most animals will become infested. The affected animal swallows the creamy-yellow eggs when grooming the body by licking and the larvae migrate to the stomach. There they stay for ten to twelve months and mature in the following spring or early summer when they become detached and are passed in the faeces. In the stomach, bots can cause inflammation, digestive disorders and colic, but despite most animals having bots, this is thought to be quite a rare occurrence. It is best to wait until December to treat the parasite, by which time they will be in the stomach and frosts will have killed the bot flies.

Warbles – Hypoderma spp. Warble flies have been eradicated in the UK. In other countries the adult flies lay eggs in the summer months from which larvae (warbles) migrate to reappear as skin nodules in the saddle area in the following spring and summer. These can be palpated as distinct swellings from which the pupae emerge to adulthood to recommence the cycle. The parasite is classified as 'erratic', which means it is not especially significant, and trials in the USA show that it can be controlled with 'pour-on' insecticides like those used for cattle.

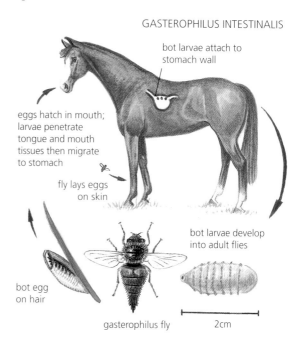

GASTEROPHILUS INTESTINALIS

bot larvae attach to stomach wall

eggs hatch in mouth; larvae penetrate tongue and mouth tissues then migrate to stomach

fly lays eggs on skin

bot larvae develop into adult flies

bot egg on hair

gasterophilus fly   2cm

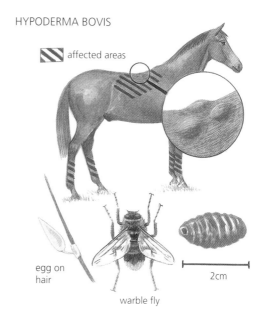

HYPODERMA BOVIS

affected areas

egg on hair

warble fly   2cm

HOW TO TELL IF YOUR HORSE HAS WORMS

The classic symptoms of a worm burden in a horse are:

- A loss in condition, anaemia, dull coat and a pot-belly.
- With severe loss in condition, there will be weakness and lethargy, which is often accompanied by fluid-filled legs and sheath and a fluid line along the lower abdomen, which 'pits' when finger pressure is applied.
- Diarrhoea – often very watery with dehydration.
- Colic – may be severe and sometimes fatal.
- Worms occasionally will be seen in droppings, but this is not a reliable indicator of a worm burden.
- Coughing might be caused by lungworms or larvae migrating through lung tissue.

Despite this list it can be very difficult to tell if your horse has a significant worm burden just by looking at it, as all these symptoms could be unrelated to internal parasites. One way of finding out if a horse is heavily parasitised is to have a faecal worm egg count done on fresh droppings. This is quite a simple test and comparatively inexpensive, and will tell an owner how many worm eggs

Keep a close watch for a loss of condition and a pot-belly.

are being passed in the droppings. During the summer months it is not uncommon for a horse to be passing many hundreds of worm eggs per gram of faeces. If a horse is passing only 100 eggs per gram of faeces (a comparatively small number) and has a faecal output of, say, 10 kg of dung in a day, it could be contaminating the pasture with up to one million eggs daily. While this test is very useful during the summer to monitor worm burdens and measure the effectiveness of worm treatments and drug resistance it does have limitations as during the winter immature and encysted strongyles will not be detected (worm egg counts could be zero) and test results may not show how many parasites

A dry, stary coat could be a sign of worms. A healthy coat should be glossy, not dull.

Watch out for fluid-filled legs.

are in the horse.

Tapeworm segments can be seen in the dung but this is not a reliable guide to infection with this parasite. A blood test has been developed that looks for tapeworm antibodies, and it's a very accurate test. This test can prove very cost-effective, for if the result is negative the horse will not need to have tapeworm treatment for at least six months because it is only necessary to treat infected horses.

There is no specific blood test for other worms but a general health blood test will give a good indication. A vet or clinical pathologist will be required to interpret general haematology and biochemistry blood results, but in general terms anaemia, high eosinophils (a type of white cell) and low albumin (a protein) levels taken with clinical factors (e.g. does it look healthy?) would tend to point to a parasite problem.

Horse reacting to colic in the abdomen by kicking and looking at flank.

Coughing can be caused by parasites in the lungs.

Collecting a dung sample in suitable pot supplied by vet.

Pinching the skin to assess dehyrdation in a sick animal.

EGG COUNT RESULTS	
0–100 per gram faeces	low worm burden
100–400 per gram faeces	moderate worm burden
over 400 per gram faeces	high worm burden

Worming Programmes

Because worms become resistant to some drug treatments over several years, worming schedules have evolved to try and minimise the risk of this all-too-common problem.

Many horse owners use a three-year rotation cycle **in the summer months** using the chemically different groups: Benzimidazole, Pyrantel and Ivermectin to include Moxidectin. Drugs of the same chemical type (see opposite) can be used within this rotation, e.g. Panacur alternating with Telmin or another from the same group.

The **winter programme** (northern hemisphere) should begin in November with treatment for cyathostome larvae with Panacur Guard. This should be done even though there is evidence of drug resistance to the Benzimidazole wormers. In December/January treat for bots using a drug from the Ivermectin group or Moxidectin. In mid-February repeat the treatment for cyathostome larvae with Panacur Guard. In March use a tapeworm dose of Strongid or Pyratape or Praziquantel (Equitape) or blood-test for tapeworms. In September treat again, as in March, for tapeworms.

EXAMPLE OF THREE-YEAR ROTATION FOR SUMMER MONTHS (April–Aug northern hemisphere)		
Year 1 Use a Benzimidazole wormer every 4–6 weeks unless a drug-resistance is known by checking the effectiveness of the drug with worm egg count.	**Year 2** Use a wormer from the Pyrantel group every 4–6 weeks. Drug resistance is less likely to be a problem with this chemical.	**Year 3** Use a product from the Ivermectin group or Moxidectin every 8–10 weeks (if using Moxidectin the manufacturers state that every 13 weeks is adequate).

RECOMMENDED ANNUAL WORMING PROGRAMME

*Typically month 1 is November in northern hemisphere; May in southern hemisphere.

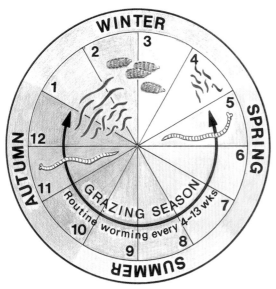

Month 1*	Treat with Panacur Guard (Fenbendazole) for 5 days against cyathostomes (alternative treatment is Moxidectin, but not as effective).
Month 2/3	Treat with drug from Ivermectin group or Moxidectin against bots.
Month 4	Repeat treatment for cyathostomes i.e. Panacur Guard or Moxidectin.
Month 5	Tapeworm treatment (Pyrantel or Praziquantel) or blood-test for tapeworms.
Months 6–10	Routine worming as per the summer programme every 4–13 weeks depending on treatment used (see above). This is correct if treating for tapeworms in months 5 and 11 using Pyrantel; if not (i.e. blood-test is negative for tapeworms or if only using Praziquantel) summer programme should run from months 5–11.
Month 11	Tapeworm treatment or blood-test for tapeworms.
Month 12	If recommended by vet, do early treatment for cyathostomes instead of in month 1.

WORMING TREATMENTS

Worming preparations fall into four chemically distinct groups. Some worming treatments, especially those in oral syringes, may contain two drugs from the different groups to widen the range of activity, e.g. a broad-spectrum wormer plus a tapeworm treatment.

GROUP 1
Macrocyclic Lactones
This includes all the **Ivermectin** preparations: Eqvalan, Furexel, Panomec, Equimax (also contains Praziquantel) and Zimectrin (USA only also with Praziquantel).

This group is effective against all major types of internal parasite (apart from encysted cyathostomes) with the exception of tapeworms, unless it is also incorporated with a tapeworm remedy (e.g. Praziquantel or Pyrantel).

Moxidectin (second generation Ivermectin)
This retails as Equest (now available with Praziquantel as Equimax or Quest Plus Gel – USA). Equest has the same spectrum of activity as Ivermectin drugs but in addition has a proven effectiveness against later stages of larval (encysted) cyathostomes.

GROUP 2
Pyrantel embonate and pamboate
Examples include Pyratape P and Strongid P and Strongid Care (USA). This group is very effective as broad-spectrum wormers and can be used as part of a general worming programme. At double the normal dose the product is very effective against tapeworms.

Spastic paralysis of the worms is the result of treatment and vets may be wary of using this type of drug to kill roundworms in foals if large numbers of worms are suspected, as they are more likely block the intestine if they die in this way. This, however, would be a very rare occurrence.

GROUP 3
Benzimidazoles
Examples are Panacur (Fenbendazole), Telmin, Systemax, Equitac (and there are many others). This group is still among the most commonly used wormers and also has the highest level of worm resistance. The drug acts by depriving the worms of nutrition and they become flaccid and die. Panacur Guard is a 10% Fenbendazole liquid preparation, which is given for five consecutive days and is the only effective treatment against all stages of cyathastome larvae.

GROUP 4
Praziquantel
Equitape (UK) is a highly effective drug against tapeworm only and is given as a single dose. Horses should remain stabled for three days after treatment to avoid tapeworms (which are passed in the dung) contaminating the pasture.

IMPORTANT
It is important when choosing a worming product for the first time to be aware of which chemical group to which it belongs. Drug companies are frequently producing 'new products' and it is vital to look at the chemical composition when selecting a treatment and deciding how it may fit into a worming regime. If you are not sure, ask your vet.

GIVING THE MEDICINE

Two people are better than one when giving medication to a horse.

Any medicine is expensive to buy, and it's even worse if you see your costly wormer being spat out or, if in feed, completely ignored by an otherwise greedy horse.

Getting the dose correct is the first necessity, so having a good idea of the animal's weight (not just a guess) is very important. Worming preparations are mostly sold as paste in oral syringes, or as granules or powder to be mixed with hard feed.

Syringe dosing can be very straightforward, but a difficult head-shy horse can make the process harder. Two people may be required to make sure the paste is deposited as far back in the mouth as possible. One person should hold the animal, while the other does the job of introducing the syringe into the side of the mouth and pressing the plunger at the right moment. Make sure the mouth is empty before you begin, as it is easier for the horse to expel the medication if its mouth is full of food. Don't wave the syringe under the animal's nose before you start as that might make it back off at speed. After the contents of the syringe have been given, keep the animal's head up until you are

reasonably sure it has swallowed. If all else fails, the contents of the syringe can be mixed with the horse's feed.

Worming treatments are formulated to be palatable and some can be mixed in with feed, which is straightforward if the animal is prepared to eat the medicated mixture. Many horses will know instantly if there is something different in 'breakfast', snort defiantly and refuse to eat up. There are various methods to overcome this reluctance. Most of the time the animal will not eat **not** because of the taste but because of the slightly different smell given off by the medication. Get around this by adding the drug to the bucket of feed and allowing it to stand for up to thirty minutes before feeding, during which time the slightly different odour should disappear. The same result can be achieved by keeping the medication in a refrigerator for a few hours before use. Alternatively get the animal used to eating a feed containing an ingredient with a strong smell, such as molasses, which will overwhelm any odour coming from the drug.

Panacur Guard is a white watery liquid, which is easy to mix with feed but can also be

Handling tips

- Never tie the horse up to administer a syringe dose. Use a headcollar and lead rope to control it.

- Wear a hard hat in case the horse rears.

- Don't dose in a stable with a low ceiling in case the horse rears.

- If in doubt, get help.

Never have the horse tied up when dosing with a syringe.

Never dose a horse in a stable that has a low roof – it's possible that the horse may rear to avoid his 'medicine'.

syringed straight into the mouth. If this method is employed keep the horse's head/nose up until it swallows, otherwise the liquid will run out of the mouth all too easily.

Tips for adding wormers to feed

- Feed a smaller amount of medicated food than the normal ration to try and ensure all the drug is eaten.

- Always put medicated feed in a bucket; never feed off the ground.

- Supervise the feeding to ensure the correct horse receives the correct dose and none is taken by another, more dominant animal.

When adding wormer to the feed, watch to see that the horse eats up and that another greedy horse doesn't steal the food.

Keeping the horse's head up until it swallows will prevent the wormer leaking out of its mouth.

TARGETED WORMING PROGRAMMES

Many equine veterinary surgeons and owners are now moving away from the blanket ('one size fits all') regular rotational worming schedule to a more considered targeted worming programme. This method relies heavily on faecal worm tests and blood testing for the presence of tapeworms, and animals are medicated according to results and the circumstances of the individual animal. Your veterinary surgeon ought to be closely involved in the decision-making process and will take other factors into account such as the age of the animals concerned, the history of parasite disease in the group, whether the pastures are overstocked and 'horse-sick' and whether, as in a livery yard, there is a consistent worming policy managed by one person. Also young horses will be much more likely to have a high worm burden and will contaminate grazing with worm larvae to a greater degree than older, more resistant animals.

The advantage of a targeted system is that it can be very cost-effective as worming treatments are only used on horses with proven high levels of infection, and the cost of the diagnostic tests are more than offset by the saving on the drug bill. There is a benefit to the environment in that, with the Ivermectin group in particular, residual activity of the chemical in the dung of the horse may kill many insects and worms that normally speed up the elimination of the faeces from the pasture. Using fewer drugs will also mean that with a reduced exposure to anthelmintics, worms are less likely to develop resistance.

The disadvantage of the targeted system is that for it to be really safe and effective the owner has to be proactive all the time or a really dangerous situation for the animal could develop all too easily. It could also be possible to forget to treat the animal for cyathostomes in the spring and late autumn, as they cannot be detected by current laboratory tests.

For many owners the interval treatment schedule may be the only safe option. In the long term vaccines may be developed which will immunise the animal against particular parasites, but there is nothing available at the moment.

Target the horse's individual needs. Know your horse's enemy – the internal parasite.

GOLDEN RULES FOR WORMING

1. Never under-dose. A weight-measuring band, while not perfect, is a very useful, cheap device for assessing horse and pony weights.

2. All horse and ponies on the same grazing should be wormed with the same product and at the same time.

3. Worm all new horses and then keep them off communal grazing for 2–3 days.

4. If horses are being moved to a new field, worm them on the day of the move and make a point of picking up the dung for 2–3 days.

5. If worried about resistance do a faecal egg count test. Samples are taken on the day of treatment and then again 7–21 days later. If resistance is present (i.e. the worm egg count is not significantly decreased or might even have increased) that group of wormers should not be used again during the grazing season. If resistance is proved to the Benzimidazole group of wormers this must not stop treatment for cyathostomes by Panacur Guard. The same applies for bot and tapeworm treatment with the other drugs.

6. Don't be afraid to worm a pregnant mare. All the worming groups are safe to use during pregnancy, but if in doubt ask your vet.

7. Some foals may have to be treated from 2 weeks of age (under veterinary supervision) due to infection from *Strongyloides westeri*. Otherwise start at 6–8 weeks of age and try to dose at the same time as the mother.

8. Always ask the vet before worming an ill horse. If it has a large number of worms the

Measuring the horse's girth with a weight-measuring band.

Foal suckling and potentially getting infected through the mare's milk.

sudden removal of all the worms may cause a blockage or precipitate a mass emergence of hibernating encysted larvae, both of which could be disastrous.

9. Keep a record of all medications for individual animals.

Make sure all medications are stored in a cool, dry, locked cupboard.

PARASITE PREVENTION

It's an old adage but worth repeating: 'Prevention is always cheaper and better than cure.' Anthelmintic drugs are a necessary expense for all horse and pony owners, but there is much that can be done to reduce the worm burden in the field and in the animal; moreover these measures are not only cost-effective but may not actually cost any money at all. In any event, it is unwise to rely totally on worming treatments to control parasites, as no drug medication, no matter how good, is likely to be 100% effective. **Good pasture management is just as vital as using the best worming treatments.**

- The **regular removal of dung from pasture** is the single most effective way of reducing or preventing a build-up of a worm burden in a field. It's hard work unless you are lucky enough to have a motorised suction cleaner, but well worth the effort even if it has to be by shovel and wheelbarrow. Twice a week in the summer months is usually aimed for, and once a week during the winter. This is essential to keep the

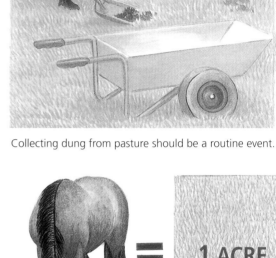

Collecting dung from pasture should be a routine event.

= 1 ACRE

Electric fencing is useful for good pasture management, especially on small acreages.

level of infective larvae as low as possible. If this isn't done the pasture will inevitably become contaminated and 'horse-sick', and probably very quickly.

- **Don't overstock.** In my opinion the ideal is one horse to one acre. Many horse owners, however, have a limited amount of grazing space and it can be very difficult to rotate fields to allow a pasture time to be cleaned and rested. It is always difficult to know how long to rest a field. Six to eight weeks is the absolute minimum time to clean a seriously dirty paddock. Pasture should be rested for at least six months, but a year would be better. This, however, is often not practical in many situations. Very horse-sick fields may have to be ploughed and reseeded.

When the horse(s) are to be moved to clean grazing, worm first and then pick up the dung in the new pasture for three days (or stable for three days). The same applies when introducing a new horse to communal grazing.

If grazing is limited and only one field is available use an electric fence to partition off part of it. This is a useful technique for good pasture management and cheaper than erecting post and rail fencing. It is very common to overstock horses, especially in the winter months when using turn-out paddocks. If this is the case collect the dung daily as you would in the stables. If time is scarce during the short days of winter concentrate on removing dung from paddocks where the youngsters are turned out, as they are more at risk. Foals and yearlings are always at much higher risk from contaminated grazing than are older animals.

In an ideal world younger animals should only be exposed to very clean pasture as infection by even a few thousand larvae could be catastrophic due to the animals' immune system not being fully developed.

- **Mixed grazing**, using cattle and sheep, can be very useful for reducing pasture contamination. Sheep and cattle eat the horse worms – and vice versa – and there is no cross-over of infection. Ruminants are also very effective at improving the quality of the grass, as they will eat much of the coarse grass that most horses will reject. Topping the rank grass with a mower does improve grass quality but does not reduce the worm burden. Turning animals out into a field that has been rested and then cut for hay is a very effective use of resources.

- Try to **avoid wet, badly drained fields**. Parasites like wet pastures.

- **Harrowing** a field when it is wet is disastrous as this will spread infective worms all over the pasture and probably increase the risks to the grazing animals. During a hot, dry spell of weather in the summer months harrowing can be effective at breaking up dung and exposing eggs and larvae to sunshine, which will kill off a lot of infection. Harrowing is a useful technique for improving grass quality but unless a good spell of hot, dry weather is guaranteed then the dung should be removed first.

- If feeding hay or hard feed in a paddock, **avoid feeding off the ground**.

- It is possible to avoid bot infestation by removing bot eggs daily with a bot knife during the fly season (from July to September in the UK) and using a fly repellent, but these measures are unlikely to be totally effective and a winter dose from the Ivermectin group should not be neglected.

- **Thoroughly cleaning a stable** – perhaps

steam cleaning once a year and leaving the building to dry thoroughly – will destroy any residual parasite eggs.

- Get rid of pinworms by **sponge cleaning the dock** area regularly.

- If you keep your horse in a yard with many different horses and owners, try to reach an agreement, after consultation with the yard vet, to **establish a common schedule** for prevention and treatment of internal parasites. In this way, treatments are far more effective and drug resistance will be kept as low as possible.

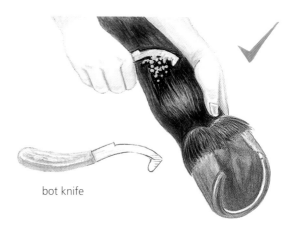

bot knife

Golden rules for parasite prevention

- Remove dung from pasture, stables and stalls.

- Do not over-populate paddocks and make sure they are all well drained.

- Avoid ground feeding.

- Routinely check horses for signs of parasite infection.

- Make sure a new horse is wormed with Moxidectin at least 3 days before introducing it to common grazing. Alternatively dose with Panacur Guard for 5 days, then wait a further 3 days before introduction to the field.

- Establish a worm prevention and monitoring programme in conjunction with your vet.

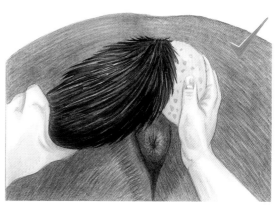

CONCLUSION

In a normal environment there can be no such thing as a worm-free horse. Sterile laboratory conditions could produce and keep a horse worm-free but the animal would not be able to go outside, graze and interact with other horses. The aim of drug treatment and prevention measures is to stop horses becoming heavily infected with parasites, which is dangerous to the health of the animal and spreads infection to others. Most adult equines can tolerate a low worm burden and have a healthy immune system. Many animals with high levels of parasitism may look unwell but many do not, and it is often impossible to decide whether your horse has a problem without doing a faecal worm count and a blood test. The incidence of colic-related deaths is apparently dropping, and this may in part be due to the increased efficacy of worming treatments and control measures. Horse owners in general are much more aware than just a few years ago about the perils of parasitism, but continual vigilance and care is essential to ensure your animal does not become one of the victims.

As long as there are horses there will be worms, but a caring, thinking owner is the horse's best protection against parasites.